Granley Elementary

2034987

Pioneers of the frontier / Charles W. Sund...

FRONTIER LAND

PIONEERS

OF THE FRONTIER

Charles W. Sundling

Visit us at
www.abdopub.com

Published by ABDO Publishing Company, 4940 Viking Drive, Edina, MN 55435.
Copyright ©2000 by Abdo Consulting Group, Inc. International copyrights
reserved in all countries. No part of this book may be reproduced in any form
without written permission from the publisher.

Printed in the United States.

Edited by: Tamara L. Britton
Art Direction: John Hamilton

Cover photo: Corbis-Bettmann
Interior photos: Corbis-Bettmann

Sources: Adams, Alexander B. *Sunlight and Storm: The Great American West.*
New York: Putnam and Sons, 1977; *American Heritage History of the Great
West, The.* New York: American Heritage, 1965; Brown, Dee. *Hear That Lone-
some Whistle Blow.* New York: Holt, Rhinehart and Winston, 1977; Dillinger,
William C. *The Gold Discovery.* Sacramento, 1990; Encarta 98 Desk Encyclope-
dia, 1996-97, Microsoft Corporation, 1996; Encyclopedia Britannica, Chicago:
Encyclopedia Britannica, Inc., 1993; Grolier Multimedia Encyclopedia, The
1995, Grolier Electronic Publishing, 1995; Holbrook, August. *Story of American
Railroads.* Crown Publishing, 1947; Lamar, Howard (editor). *The Reader's
Encyclopedia of the Old West.* New York, 1977; Milner, Clyde A. et. al. (editors).
The Oxford History of the American West. New York, 1990.

Library of Congress Cataloging–in–Publication Data

Sundling, Charles W.
    Pioneers of the frontier / Charles W. Sundling
        p. cm. — (Frontier land)
    Includes index.
    Summary: Describes what life was like for some of the pioneers who went
west during the second half of the nineteenth century to prospect for gold, build
railroads, and settle the Great Plains.
    ISBN 1-57765-047-6
    1. Pioneers—West (U.S.)—History—Juvenile literature. 2. Frontier and
pioneer life—West (U.S.)—Juvenile literature. 3. West (U.S.)—History—
Juvenile literature. [1. Pioneers. 2. Frontier and pioneer life—West (U.S.)
3. West (U.S.)—History.]
I. Title. II. Series: Sundling, Charles W. Frontier land.
F596.S933 2000
978—DC21
                                                    98-6606
                                                        CIP
                                                         AC

CONTENTS

SUTTER'S SECRET

Gold is a very special metal. It's strong, durable, and also malleable, which means it is easily shaped or formed. Gold can be made into a thin thread or pounded into paper-thin sheets. All of these properties make gold very valuable.

Early Spanish explorers came to America in search of gold. They believed part of America was a land of gold that they called "El Dorado." Explorers Hernando de Soto, Francisco Valasquez de Coronado, and others looked for El Dorado, but they never found it.

In early 1848, Johann (John) Augustus Sutter, an immigrant from Switzerland, owned a ranch in the Sacramento Valley of California. He had hired a carpenter to build a new sawmill. One day, the carpenter noticed shiny chips of metal in a ditch. Sutter and the carpenter tested the chips. They were gold.

Sutter wasn't happy about the discovery. He wanted to keep the gold a secret. Sutter had acquired his ranch when California was a Mexican province. But California had become a part of the United States, and was being governed by a transitional government.

Sutter tried to get mineral rights so he could claim the gold that was on his land. But Sutter could not get the mineral rights until Mexico and the United States signed the treaty of Guadalupe-Hidalgo.

Sutter's Mill, site of the discovery of gold in California.

In three months the news of gold on Sutter's ranch reached San Francisco. Three out of every four men left San Francisco for Sutter's ranch. The news quickly spread to other California towns. By July of 1848, more than 3,000 men had arrived to seek gold on Sutter's ranch.

In December 1848, United States President James K. Polk said that the hills of California contained a lot of gold. As proof, 230 ounces (6.5 kg) were placed on public display. Sutter soon lost his ranch when thousands of gold seekers descended on his land and took it over.

BY SEA OR BY LAND?

In 1849, America was gold crazy. People abandoned their homes, jobs, and families to go California, encouraged by tales of abundant wealth. Rumors were repeated as if they were true stories. People said that California's rivers ran with water and gold. They said that a person could easily find $1,000 in gold each day of the week. They said that one man dipped his hat in a river and found a gold nugget.

Thousands of people wanted to find gold and get rich in California. These gold hunters were known as Forty-Niners, or the Argonauts of '49. Most of the Forty-Niners came from the eastern United States. Others came from Mexico, China, and South America.

Traveling by ship was the easiest way to get from the eastern United States to California. Ships left the East Coast, went around South America, then sailed to California. This route was almost 15,000 miles (24,135 km) long. Sea trips could take as long as six months to complete.

There was another route that was shorter. Ships left the East Coast and went to Panama. But, the Panama Canal did not open for traffic until 1914. So the Forty-Niners left

A park ranger wears 1800s-style clothing like that of pioneers traveling the Oregon Trail. Dome Rock stands in the background. Dome Rock was a famous landmark to pioneers traveling west on the Oregon and Mormon Trails from the 1800s to the 1930s.

the ships and trekked across the narrowest part of Panama on land. On the Pacific side of Panama, they boarded other ships headed for California.

The sea trips were dangerous. Wild storms were often encountered, and many Forty-Niners died in shipwrecks. Forty-Niners on the sea trips drank stale water. They also ate bad food. Sometimes the bread was moldy and had insects living in it. Nevertheless, thousands of Forty-Niners came to California by ship.

More Forty-Niners came to California by overland routes. Some followed the Oregon Trail from Independence, Missouri, to Portland, Oregon. Some followed the Mormon Trail from Nauvoo, Illinois, to Salt Lake City, Utah. Most of these Forty-Niners were town and city people. They had never lived in the outdoors. A lot of Forty-Niners died because of their ignorance of the outdoors.

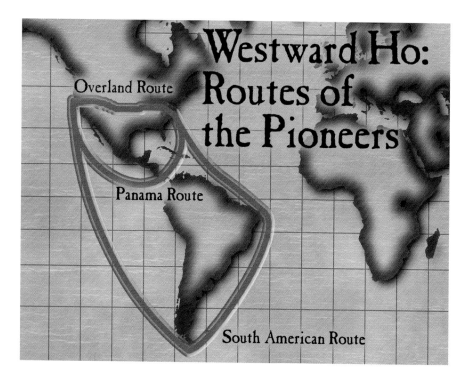

A prospector pans for gold in a mountain stream.

GOLD MINING

Many of the first gold seekers were placer miners. Placer mining was cheap—prospectors took gravel and dirt from a stream and tossed it into a pan. They added water, then swirled the mixture around, letting it spill out over the sides. The water washed the gravel and dirt away, leaving the heavy gold at the bottom of the pan.

Placer mining, also called panning for gold, was slow work. Prospectors wanted to find gold faster, so they began using cradles, or rockers. Cradles had iron tops with holes in them, and ridges inside on the bottom. Miners shoveled dirt and gravel into the cradle and then added water. When the cradle was rocked, the water took the dirt and gravel away. The gold stayed inside, trapped behind the ridges.

Prospectors also used a device called a Long Tom. This was a 20-foot (6.1 m) trench, made of wood, 18 inches (46 cm) deep, with ridges built into its inner walls. Prospectors put Long Toms in streams so that water ran through them. Then they placed gravel and dirt into the Long Toms. The water carried the gravel and dirt away, while gold stayed in the ridges.

Two miners of the California gold rush use a cradle to separate gold from soil.

A prospector uses a Long Tom, a device to wash the gold from gold-bearing soil.

To find gold even faster, prospectors also used sluice boxes, which resembled a long line of Long Toms. The bottoms of the boxes had ridges to catch the gold. Prospectors put one end of the sluice box in a stream. Men shoveled gravel and dirt into the sluice boxes. Water carried the gravel and dirt away, but the heavier gold stayed in the ridges. Several men were needed to work a sluice box.

When most of the gold had been taken from a river or stream, prospectors began looking for the source of the gold in the adjoining hills. Prospectors dug tunnels in the hills. Then they used picks and shovels to break up rock, and the broken rock was taken out of the tunnels in carts that were pulled by mules. At the surface, the rock was crushed and the gold was separated from it.

A mule pulls a cart through this late-nineteenth century California gold mine.

The gold that was easy to find was gone by the time prospectors resorted to digging tunnels in the hills. More money was needed to find the gold that was locked in the rocks. The individual prospectors did not have the money, but big companies did. They hired men to dig long ditches or build long wooden gutters or troughs. These ditches or troughs were called flumes. Water flowed down the flumes, went through hoses, and then into long-barreled cannons. The men shot the water at the rocks, breaking up the ore and making the gold easier to find. Companies called this hydraulic mining.

Hydraulic mining ruined the land. Hills collapsed and forests died. Dirt and other material ran into the rivers and streams. In 1884, California declared hydraulic mining illegal, but by then the California gold rush was over.

After the gold rush, some prospectors went home, while others worked in foundries, shops, factories, or became farmers. Some prospectors continued mining for gold. They rushed to Nevada, Colorado, Montana, Alaska, and the Black Hills of South Dakota. Few ever became rich.

This prospector uses hydraulic mining to break up the hillside and make gold easier to find.

A train pulls into the station of a town on the Western frontier.

RAILROAD ACROSS AMERICA

In 1862, President Abraham Lincoln signed the Pacific Railroad Act. Its goal was to build a railroad line across the vast expanse of the American West. Two companies were chartered to build the line: The Central Pacific Railroad Company and the Union Pacific Railroad Company. The Union Pacific would start at the eastern end and the Central Pacific would start at the western end. The plan was to have them meet somewhere in the middle. And when that happened, as railroad employee Arthur Ferguson wrote, "There will be no West." What he meant was that when the two rail lines finally linked the country together, the West would be changed forever.

The Union Pacific Railroad started laying track in Omaha, Nebraska, on the western shore of the Missouri River, which was considered the gateway to the American frontier. The company employed thousands of immigrant workers and Civil War veterans to lay track on the new line. Working west across the Great Plains, the Union Pacific Railroad workers had mostly flat land for laying track. Still, the work could be difficult and dangerous.

The Central Pacific Railroad began its line in Sacramento, California. Working eastward, the work crews soon came upon a seemingly impassable obstacle—the Sierra Nevada Mountains. Many believed that this steep and

dangerous mountain range could never be crossed by railroad, but the Central Pacific succeeded by constructing bridges and wooden trestles over canyons, blasting narrow ledges on the sides of mountains, and boring tunnels through solid rock. Thousands of hard-working Chinese immigrants eventually made up about 90 percent of the Central Pacific's work force.

Workers driving spikes into railroad ties.

A train passes through the 800-foot (244 m) long Bloomer Cut, carved through the Sierra Nevada Mountains by Central Pacific work crews.

Chinese workers put the finishing touches on a train trestle nestled in the Sierra Nevada Mountains.

To build the railroad, workers first constructed a road-bed by leveling the ground and slanting its sides downward. The slanted sides caused rain to run off the roadbed. Next they put railroad ties on the roadbed. Then workers placed the iron rails on top of the ties. The rails were joined end to end with braces called fishplates, and connected to the ties with spikes. Depending on the terrain, a work crew could lay about one mile (1.6 km) of track per day.

In addition to the dangers of the work itself, railroad crews had to contend with hostile Native Americans, who rightly saw the coming railway as a threat to their way of

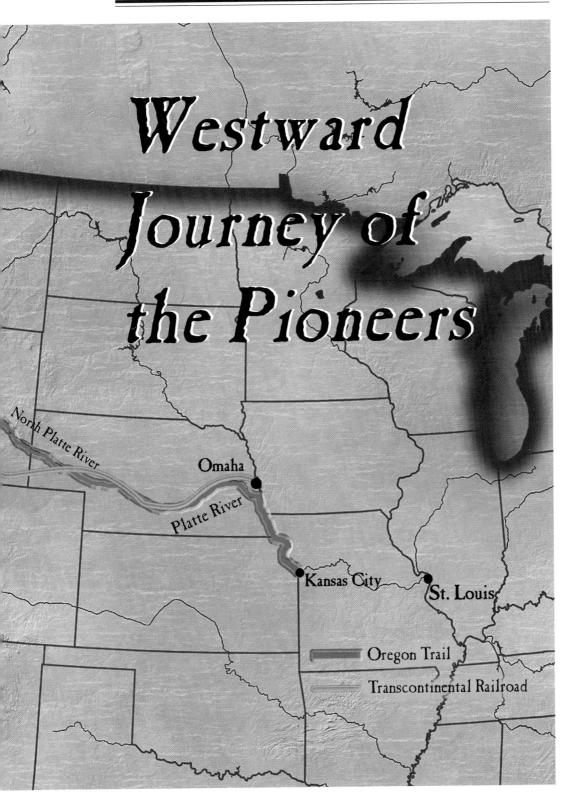

Westward Journey of the Pioneers

North Platte River

Omaha

Platte River

Kansas City

St. Louis

Oregon Trail

Transcontinental Railroad

A group of Native Americans attack Union Pacific Railroad workers on a hand-car.

life. Bad weather was another danger. The winter of 1866-1867 was terrible in the Sierra Nevada Mountains and on the Great Plains. In the Sierras, a series of blizzards struck, killing hundreds of workers in avalanches and sub-zero temperatures.

As the Union Pacific moved west across the plains, "tent towns" followed the work crews. Tent towns were hastily set up towns of tents and wood shanties. The people who set up the tent towns wanted to make money. The railroad workers went into the towns to relax. They spent their money at restaurants, bakeries, saloons, and billiard rooms. Most tent towns disappeared when the railroad workers moved on down the line. But some tent towns, such as Cheyenne, Wyoming, and Grand Island, Nebraska, became permanent settlements.

In early 1869, the rail lines of both the Central Pacific and the Union Pacific had reached Utah. Congress had never told the companies exactly where the tracks should join. President Ulysses S. Grant finally ordered the companies to select a location to join the tracks. The companies decided to link the tracks at Promontory Point, Utah.

On May 10, 1869, workers laid the last tie and the last two rails. Officials of both railroads hammered ceremonial spikes into the last rail. There was a silver spike from the Comstock Lode in Nevada, a gold-silver-iron alloy spike from the governor of Arizona, and a golden spike donated by David Hewes of San Francisco. The Central Pacific's locomotive *Jupiter* and the Union Pacific's locomotive *Number 119* pulled so close together that their cowcatchers almost touched. The transcontinental railroad was finally complete.

On May 10, 1869, a golden spike was driven at Promontory Point, Utah, symbolizing the joining of the Central Pacific and Union Pacific lines.

BREAKING A BARRIER

The Great Plains went from Montana and the Dakotas all the way south to Texas. Rain was not plentiful on the plains. Few trees grew there. Stephen Long, an early explorer, said people could never farm the plains. He called the Great Plains the Great American Desert.

Two things finally broke the Great Plains barrier. The first were the railroads. The United States government granted the railroads more land than they needed for their tracks. This land could be sold to people who would settle on farms, or in towns along the railroad tracks.

To attract people to settle near the tracks, railroad companies bragged about their land. They said that railroads made it rain more, that "rain follows the plow." Some scientists at the time thought farming brought more rain.

In addition, farmers would need to send their crops on the railroads. Businesses would receive supplies sent on the railroads. The railroads would make a lot of money, and this gave them a big incentive to lay as much track across the West as possible.

The other thing that helped break the Great Plains barrier was the Homestead Act of 1862. The government sold land for a $10 filing fee. Nearly everybody could receive

Pioneers like the family shown here in front of their sod home in Custer County, Nebraska, left the East to settle in frontier country. Between 1862 and 1900, around 400,000 families received cheap land from the government under the Homestead Act.

160 acres of land. A person had to be at least 21 years old and a United States citizen, or have plans to become a citizen. After living on the land for five years, the homesteader gained full title to his or her property.

Americans came in droves to the Great Plains to take advantage of the Homestead Act. Thousands of European immigrants wanted homestead land, too. Many farmers in Europe never owned the land they worked on. The Homestead Act was a chance for them to own their own farms.

Unfortunately, most of the new settlers were unaware of how harsh conditions could be on the Great Plains. In summer, high temperatures could rise past 100 degrees Fahren-heit (38 degrees Celsius). Rain might not fall for weeks. Prairie fires swept across the dry land, burning everything in their path.

In the summer of 1874, millions of grasshoppers ate entire fields of crops in a matter of hours. One farmer claimed that "they looked like a great, white glistening cloud, for their wings caught the sunshine on them and made them look like a cloud of vapor." Because of the grass-hopper plague, trains sometimes had to stop; crushed grass-hoppers made the tracks slippery, causing trains to derail.

Winters on the Great Plains weren't any easier for the settlers. High temperatures might stay below zero degrees Fahrenheit (-18 degrees Celsius) for days at a time. The low temperatures might fall to -40 degrees Fahrenheit (-40 degrees Celsius). On January 12, 1888, a blizzard came up suddenly on what had been a warm day. It struck in the afternoon when children were leaving school to walk home. Many children became disoriented in the whirling snow and died when they could not reach shelter. This blizzard be-came known as the "Schoolchildren's Blizzard."

But the weather could also be kind on the Great Plains, with mild temperatures in both winter and summer. Some-times enough summer rain might fall to grow large crops, and an entire winter might go by without a single blizzard. The new settlers learned that the weather in the Great Plains was uncertain.

The settlers, however, knew one thing for certain: they needed shelter. Dugouts were easy shelters to build. Settlers simply dug out part of a hill, then stacked thick pieces of sod to make a front wall. If wood was available, it was used to

Dust storms on the Great Plains, like this one over Midland, Texas, on February 20, 1894, could blow acres of soil away.

make the dugout's roof. If wood was scarce, thick pieces of sod were used to finish the roofs.

Sod houses, or "soddies," were another common shelter on the Great Plains. Settlers used sod, or "prairie marble," for shelters. They cut thick pieces of sod from the ground and stacked them like bricks. Sod houses were cheap to build, were warm in winter and cool in summer, and were also bulletproof and fireproof.

However, sod houses were dark and damp. After a rain storm, water dripped from the ceilings. Many times insects and snakes fell from the ceiling. Yet, settlers built thousands of sod houses. They built so many that people called the Great Plains "the sod house frontier."

An old wooden windmill on the vast Great Plains.

FARMING A HOMESTEAD

After building their shelter, most homesteaders began farming. The first thing they needed was a good source of water to irrigate their crops, and to drink, wash, and cook with. But water could be scarce, and some farmers needed to dig wells.

Some homesteaders dug their own wells. Many hired expert well diggers. Sometimes well diggers found water just below the ground. Occasionally they had to dig several hundred feet to find water. Many times farmers bought or made windmills. The wind turned a pump, which brought the well water to the surface.

The prairie sod, with its thick grassy roots, was difficult to plow. Homesteaders had to use sharp, hard steel plows to cut the sod. When homesteaders plowed the ground, the dirt dried quickly. Light winds easily blew dry dirt away. "Dry farming" involved plowing the fields after a rain, which turned the soil over and kept the dirt moist.

Homesteaders planted different crops in different parts of the Great Plains. Flax and wheat grew well in some places, while corn grew well in others. Homesteaders planted the crops that grew best on their land.

Farmers on a homestead had to provide for all of their families' needs. Sometimes there was a good harvest and the farmers had surplus food and grain to sell or trade. Then they could get supplies from the store. But if the

Cows and windmill in west Texas.

harvest was small or the crops failed, everything a family needed had to be produced on the farm. Not only did they need to grow all of their food, they had to grow food for their animals, too. Vegetables, fruits, and meats had to be preserved for use during winter. Homesteaders weaved cloth and made their own clothing. Soap and candles were home-made, too.

Homesteading was a tough life. Many homesteaders eventually quit and returned to their old homes. However, more and more people kept coming. Everybody, it seemed, wanted his or her 160 acres of land. With determination, hard work, and more than a little luck, these hardy pioneers turned the Great American Desert into the productive farmland that it is today.

A portrait of Old West pioneers from Telluride, Colorado.

INTERNET SITES

http://www.uprr.com/uprr/ffh/history/

The history section of the official Web site of the Union Pacific Railroad includes a detailed history of the railroad. The site also gives biographical information on significant individuals who helped start the company and worked on the first transcontinental railroad.

http://memory.loc.gov/ammem/cbhtml/ cbintro.html

"California As I Saw It" is a Web site created by the Library of Congress in Washington, D.C. It documents the formative era of California's history through eyewitness accounts. The collection covers the dramatic decades between the California gold rush and the turn of the twentieth century.

These sites are subject to change. Go to your favorite search engine and type in "pioneers" for more sites.

PASS IT ON

History buffs: educate readers around the country by passing on information you've learned about early-American pioneers. Share your little-known facts and interesting stories. We want to hear from you!

To get posted on the ABDO Publishing Company Web site, email us at "History@abdopub.com"

**Visit the ABDO Publishing Company Web site at:
www.abdopub.com**

GLOSSARY

Argonaut: An adventurer engaged in a quest.

Claim office: An authority that keeps records of land ownership.

Continent: A large mass of land, such as Europe, Asia, or North America.

Cowcatcher: a frame on the front of a train used to throw things off the track that got in the way of the train.

Cradle: A prospecting device that looks like a baby's rocker.

Dry farming: A method of farming that prevents soil erosion.

El Dorado: A Spanish term meaning "land of gold." The Spanish believed El Dorado was in America.

Flume: A long wooden gutter that carries water.

Forty-Niners: People who went to California in 1849 to search for gold.

Great Plains: The land from Canada to the Gulf of Mexico and from the Mississippi River to the Rocky Mountains.

Long Tom: A gold prospecting device similar to a *cradle*, but longer and placed in the water.

Placer: A Spanish word that is pronounced "plah-sir."

The word means gravel beds. Placer mining is also called panning for gold.

Prairie marble: Sod blocks used to build houses on the prairie.

Prospector: One who hunts for gold.

Roadbed: The area where a railroad track is laid.

Sluice box: A long line of wooden boxes joined together. The boxes have ridges on their bottoms to catch gold.

Sod: The top layer of ground on a prairie. It is made up of grass and weeds and their roots.

Spike: A heavy nail used to hold railroad rails to wooden ties.

Tent town: Temporary town made of tents where Union Pacific workers lived.

Ties: Wooden beams laid across a railroad bed. The track is secured to the ties.

Veteran: A person who has fought or served in a war.

A freight car passes through a tunnel dug out after the "Big Snow" of 1880.

INDEX